Contents

Adapt and survive!

In the struggle for survival, the fittest win out at the expense of their rivals because they succeed in adapting themselves best to their environment.

Charles Darwin, Scientist

Living things need air, water and food to survive. They also need protection from predators. Plants and animals thrive and exist together with other species in their native habitats because they have adapted to the conditions of the environment.

Plants and animals have a variety of physical **characteristics** and behaviours to protect them from being eaten, including hiding, **camouflage**, protective coverings, and living in large groups.

All living things are closely related to their environment. Any change in one part of an environment causes a ripple effect of changes in other parts of the environment. When this happens, the balance of nature is altered and only animals or plants that adapt will survive. Those that don't, face extinction.

Did you know?
The main reasons a chameleon changes colour are a change in body temperature or to send a message to other animals. A brightly coloured chameleon is very warm or very angry!

LET'S FIND OUT

- Why do plants and animals adapt to changes in their environment?
- Why do humans have a responsibility to minimise their impact on nature?
- What are some different types of adaptations?
- How does human development affect environments?
- Why do we need to prevent species of plants and animals from becoming extinct?

characteristics features that can be used to name something
camouflage ability to blend in with the background

This chameleon is either very warm or very angry.

Adapting to change

Living things can adapt to changes in their environment in order to survive. The main threats to survival are temperature, lack of food or water, and predators. In any environment, the **flora** and **fauna** have adapted to the conditions.

Physical adaptations

Adaptations can take many forms. Camels have adapted physically and behaviourally so they can walk in the desert. They have broad, flat, leathery feet with two toes on each foot. When a camel walks, the pads on its feet spread so that the feet don't sink into the sand. Also, the camel moves both feet on one side of its body, then both feet on the other.

Desert plants have adapted to the harsh environment, too. The creosote bush produces poisons that stop other plants from growing close to it. This gives the bush a larger area to itself, so it can get more nutrients and water from the soil.

Blending in

Some adaptations are astonishing *and* practical. Some insects and plants blend into their surroundings to avoid predators. When motionless, a stick insect is identical to a stick, and a katydid looks exactly like a leaf.

Lithops (or stone plants) look like pebbles, to protect themselves.

These are some of the ways that plants and animals have adapted to survive.

The creosote bush produces poison to keep other plants away.

A katydid looks like a dried-up leaf.

flora the plants native to a particular area
fauna the animals native to a particular area

Breakaway tasks

Remembering

1 List the main threats to survival for plants and animals.

2 Describe how camels have adapted so that they can walk in the desert.

Understanding

3 Write five True or False statements about the animals and plants in the text. Then swap your quiz with a classmate.

4 Explain why a katydid would benefit from looking like a leaf.

Applying

5 Research and find facts about other adaptations that allow camels to live in deserts. Use your information to write a fact file.

6 Research another animal or plant not mentioned in the information report. Then create a poster describing the ways it has adapted to its environment.

Analysing

7 Write another paragraph to add to the report about how animals and plants have adapted to changes caused by humans.

8 Write and deliver a speech or debate to your class on the topic:
'Which is the bigger threat: human development or predators?'

Evaluating

9 Write a report to describe how you have adapted to fit into the school environment.

Creating

10 Write a narrative based on one of the adaptions in the information report. Include illustrations. Read your story to another class.

Operation axolotl

Day 1

I'm in Mexico City, which is ages away from Perth (see the map). I'm with my mum and she's studying the Mexican **salamander**, or axolotl (say *ak-suh-lo-tl*), with a university research team. Here's a photo of my pet axolotl, Smiley. He's too cute!

I'm going to help Mum find out about the axolotls in Lake Xochimilco (*so-chee-mill-koh*), the only place where they exist in the wild.

I discovered there's an **Aztec** legend about a god who thought the other gods were going to kill him. He escaped by changing himself into a new water creature that the Aztecs could eat. The people were

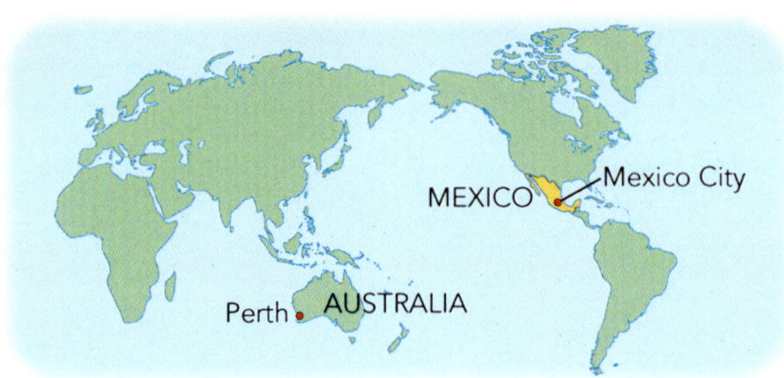

very grateful for this new food and called it *axolotl*, which means 'water monster'.

Day 2

Here are some facts about axolotls:

- **Lifespan:** about 12–15 years, but can live up to 25 years
- **Size:** average length of 23 cm but can grow up to 45 cm
- **Weight:** between 60 and 230 g
- **Diet:** they're **carnivores**, eating earthworms, insects, small fish, shellfish and tadpoles.
- Axolotls are different from other salamanders. They remain in the larva stage, even when they grow to adulthood and can breed. (Larva stage means living in water and breathing through gills.)

More on this tomorrow.

salamander a small animal that lives on land and in water
Aztec indigenous people of Central Mexico
carnivores animals that eat meat

Day 3

More facts about axolotls:

- They have large flat heads, gills, and small limbs with long **digits**.
- They are popular as pets, living in a tank. The water temperature must be 14–18°C. They are most active in the evening.
- Their teeth grip, rather than bite or tear. They swallow their food whole.

Here's an axolotl's life cycle.

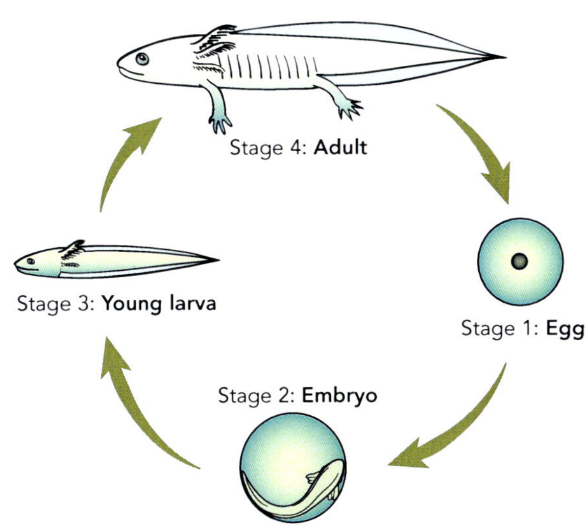

Day 4

Today I found out some worrying statistics. Between 1998 and 2008, the number of axolotls in the wild was reduced by 98%! They are now extremely endangered! There are several reasons for this.

1. The axolotls' native habitat is being reduced, because parts of Lake Xochimilco have been drained.
2. The lake is polluted.
3. Tilapia fish (see my pic) have been **introduced** for the people of Mexico City to catch and eat. But the tilapias eat the plants that axolotls lay their eggs on.
4. Axolotls are still eaten as a treat.

A tilapia

Day 5

Biologists have different ideas about how to save the axolotl. Some think the axolotl should be preserved only in its natural environment.

digits fingers or toes
introduced bring a new plant or creature into a habitat
biologists people who study living organisms

Biologists have looked at repopulating Lake Xochimilco with axolotls reared in **captivity**. This is risky because they might have **parasites** and viruses or inherited problems.

Some biologists promote traditional methods of farming. They are grinding up tilapia to make organic fertiliser to use for farming, instead of using chemicals that pollute the lake. They are also creating small tilapia-free sanctuaries by blocking off the entrances to some canals.

Other biologists say axolotls can survive in the wild, only if they are introduced into new environments. A team of researchers has begun trialling a new home in an artificial lake in Tecámac, outside Mexico City.

Day 6

Mum told me that Professor Roy of Montreal University, Canada, is studying axolotls in a lab to find out more about **regeneration**. Axolotls can regrow parts of their bodies such as tails, legs, and heart and brain tissue numerous times – and they're always perfect, with no scarring.

Professor Roy hopes his studies will one day improve tissue healing for burn victims, improve organ transplants, and might even help people with cancer. All axolotls are amazing, not just Smiley!

captivity being held in places like zoos or aquariums
parasites plants or animals that live in (or on) another species
regeneration regrowing lost or damaged parts of a body

Breakaway tasks

Remembering

1 Name the axolotl's only remaining natural habitat, and list the threats to the axolotl's survival.

2 Give examples of body parts that axolotls can grow back.

Understanding

3 Explain how axolotls are different from other salamanders.

4 In your own words, write what might happen if scientists repopulate Lake Xochimilco with axolotls reared in captivity.

Applying

5 Research information about keeping an axolotl as a pet. Design an information sheet that a pet shop owner could give to customers who purchase an axolotl.

6 Discuss the negative impacts humans have on axolotls in their natural environment. List two other animals or plants, and describe how they are affected by human development.

Analysing

7 Research another salamander and draw its life cycle.

8 Debate the following: 'Axolotls should or should not be used for medical research'.

Evaluating

9 Compare the opinions of the biologists who are working to save the axolotl from extinction in the wild. Which method do you think is most likely to be successful? Justify your answer.

Creating

10 Write your own legend about the first axolotl, describing how such a creature came to exist.

11 Plan an advertising campaign to protect and prevent the extinction of axolotls in the wild.

Adapting to Australian environments

Australian animals

Name and environment:	Structural features and adaptations:
Thorny devil lizard — desert dweller, central Australia 	• It doesn't sweat or lose water through its skin. • Its body is covered in scales with grooves between them. The grooves catch rainwater and dew that the lizard can suck into its mouth. • Its brown colours camouflage the lizard in the desert.
Koala — tree dweller, eastern eucalypt forests 	• Its paws are designed for gripping and climbing trees. The front paws have two **opposable** digits, like the human thumb. The back paws have one digit. It has strong, sharp claws. • It does not have a tail and has dense fur on its rump, which allows it to sit comfortably in a tree.
Water-holding frog — desert dweller, central Australia 	• When it rains, the frog takes in half its body weight in water, storing it under its skin. Then it burrows about a metre into mud, shedding its skin to form a cocoon. • The frog **hibernates** until the next rain - which could be two years later - and then surfaces and repeats the cycle.

opposable can be placed opposite the fingers of the same hand
hibernates becomes inactive; stays in a resting state

Australian plants

Name and environment:	Structural features and adaptations:
Australian mulga tree — central desert 	• The leaves grow upwards. When it rains, they collect and channel rainwater along branches and down the trunk to the ground. • The roots grow close to the base of the tree. • The **taproot** grows deep into the ground. A seedling 10 cm high can have a taproot 3 m long.
Silvertop ash — south-eastern coast and tablelands 	• **Epicormic buds** are buried deep within the trunk, but the leaves on the tree stop these buds from sprouting. • After a fire, when all the leaves are gone, the epicormic buds quickly sprout, covering the tree with new leaves and branches.
Blue marble tree — rainforest 	• The **buttress roots** can be 10–12 m high. This increases the surface area of the tree, so that it can take in more carbon dioxide and release more oxygen. • In rainforests, nutrients in the soil are near the surface, so trees have shallow roots. The buttresses support the trees.

taproot a main root of a plant; small roots grow from it
epicormic buds buds that grow when parts of the tree are damaged
buttress roots large roots on all sides of a tree

Breakaway tasks

Remembering

1 When do epicormic buds of the silvertop ash sprout?

2 Describe how a thorny devil lizard's grooves help it to drink water.

Understanding

3 Explain how the koala has evolved so that it can comfortably live in a tree.

4 Draw diagrams to identify one difference between tap roots and buttress roots.

Applying

5 Research two animals and two plants from the fact files and add two more adaptations for each one.

6 Make a poster of four Australian ocean dwellers. Describe their structural features and how each one has adapted to its environment. Include images.

Analysing

7 For the plants and animals in the fact files, identify the differences and similarities in their struggle for survival.

Evaluating

8 Looking at the adaptations described in the fact files, determine the key threat or issue that each living thing faces in its environment. Discuss your ideas with a partner.

Creating

9 Write a poem about an animal's or plant's life in an Australian environment; for example, a desert or ocean environment. Present it to the class.

10 Working as a scientist, you have found a live specimen of a plant or animal that was thought to be extinct.

Write a report about how the plant or animal adapted so that it survived, rather than becoming extinct like the other members of its species.

Adapt and flourish

Cane toads were introduced into northern Queensland from Hawaii in 1935, to control the cane beetles that fed on sugar cane crops. The toads were largely unsuccessful in controlling the cane beetles, but they adapted well to their new environment and **flourished** in it.

Cane toads are tough, and eat just about anything they can swallow. Any native animal – including goannas, crocodiles, dingoes, quolls and some snakes – that eats a toad, its tadpoles or its eggs, gets poisoned.

Females can lay 8000–35 000 eggs twice a year and their young grow very quickly. They are considered a pest and have spread from Queensland to New South Wales and the Northern Territory.

So now that you know about cane toads, it's time to do your bit. Join us on the 24th of March at Toad Day Out and help protect your area from this invader!

The cane toad, its tadpoles and its eggs are poisonous.

flourished thrived; were successful

Advertisement

TOAD DAY OUT

YOUR MISSION

If you choose to accept ...

Capture the toads for interrogation, alive and unharmed

Townsville City Council invites you to join Operation Toad Day Out! This year, get together with your friends, schools or scout groups and organise your very own Operation Toad Day Out. The challenge is to capture as many cane toads as you can – but they have to be captured alive and presented unharmed. Help to protect and free your local area from this invader.

Cane toads have been a major environmental **menace** in North Queensland for decades. If left unchecked, cane toads will damage our natural habitat and threaten our local frog population. They will wipe out native animals that see the toads as prey and **succumb** to their poison.

The wet season has provided good conditions for cane toads to multiply, so there will be many of them hopping around our region – maybe even in your own backyard!

Join your local community and play your part in reducing the numbers of these pests in a **humane** way. There are great prizes to be won, including cane toad trophies and $1000 in prize money!

When: 24 March
Where: Ross River Dam Park
Time: 8:30 a.m.–12:00 p.m.

RULES AND CONDITIONS

- Toads must be ALIVE and UNHARMED.
- Only cane toads will be accepted.
- Toads must be at least 50 mm in length.
- All toads will be identified by experts to make sure that no native frogs have been brought in by mistake. All toads will then be disposed of humanely.

interrogation questioning a suspect to get information
menace a threat or danger; likely to cause harm
succumb give in; to die
humane causing no pain; sympathetic

Breakaway tasks

Remembering

1 Explain why cane toads were brought to Australia.

2 Write about the purpose of Toad Day Out.

Understanding

3 List the features that have allowed cane toads to adapt so well.

4 Discuss with a partner what you need to do to win a prize.

Applying

5 Write a paragraph to explain the result of cane toads adapting well to their new environment.

Analysing

6 Draw a cane toad and label its features. (You may need to do some further research.)

7 As a class, discuss how effective the advertisement is. Would you take part in Toad Day Out? Why or why not? Graph your results.

Evaluating

8 Research another species that has been introduced into Australia with negative impacts. Compare and contrast the methods used to control cane toads with measures used to control this species.

Creating

9 With a partner, plan and write two persuasive texts:
- for the control of cane toads
- against the control of cane toads

Present your texts as a debate and have the class vote for the most convincing one.

10 Write a narrative about catching toads on Toad Day Out.

Strands in action

Core tasks

1 Choose a region in Australia and design a garden that suits the environment.

- Include plants that are native to the environment, and that will attract native birds and animals.
- Write notes about how the different species can exist together.
- Create a model of your garden to present to the class.

2 Research an animal that has survived since prehistoric times, such as the crocodile.

- Create a diorama or poster that shows the physical characteristics of your animal, and how it has evolved and adapted.

Extra tasks

1 Research an extinct Australian plant or animal and create a time line for its extinction. Comment on your findings.

2 Create a fact file that compares adaptations in birds, focusing on the ways that their beaks and claws have evolved to suit their environment.

3 Draw a map of Australia, showing the spread of cane toads across the nation. Write about the native animals that are threatened by the toads in each area.

4 Write an article outlining the ways in which human development impacts on the native environment where you live.

Include how native plants, animals and birds have adapted to the changes humans have brought to this environment.

When doing research for your projects, always read information from several sources, think about it, and then write it in your own words. Copying other people's writing is called *plagiarism*, and it's against the law.